GW00535780

LAND SPEED RECORDS

Don Wales

SHIRE PUBLICATIONS
Bloomsbury Publishing Plc
PO Box 883, Oxford, OX1 9PL, UK
1385 Broadway, 5th Floor, New York, NY 10018, USA

E-mail: info@ospreypublishing.com
www.ospreypublishing.com

SHIRE is a trademark of Osprey Publishing Ltd

First published in Great Britain in 2018

© Don Wales, 2018

Don Wales has asserted his right under the Copyright, Designs and Patents Act, 1988, to be identified as Author of this work.

A catalogue record for this book is available from the British Library.

ISBN: PB 978 1 78442 254 7;
eBook 978 1 78442 253 0;
ePDF 978 1 78442 252 3;
XML 978 1 78442 255 4

18 19 20 21 22   10 9 8 7 6 5 4 3 2 1

Typeset by PDQ Digital Media Solutions, Bungay, UK

Printed and bound in India by Replika Press Private Ltd.

COVER IMAGE
Bluebird at Lake Eyre, 1963. Back Cover: The Wakefield trophy was awarded to Henry Segrave in 1929 by Sir Charles Cheers Wakefield after the former had driven Golden Arrow to the record-breaking speed of 231.45mph on 11 March 1929 at Daytona Beach, Florida.

TITLE PAGE IMAGE
'ThrustSSC' breaking the sound barrier with Andy Green.

CONTENTS PAGE IMAGE
The author driving his grandfather's 350hp Sunbeam on Pendine Sands, 21 July 2015, to commemorate the 90th anniversary of the first car to break the world land speed record at over 150mph.

DEDICATION
To David Tremayne, a very good friend to whom I still owe lunch, and whose previous works on this subject have been invaluable.

ACKNOWLEDGEMENTS
Pictures are acknowledged as follows:

Author's collection, pages 10, 20, 26, 27, 28, 30, 36 (top), 57; Brooklands Museum, page 13 (bottom); Nick Chapman, page 52; Sam Hawley, page 40 (bottom); Colleen Herr, page 60 (top); Matt Howell Photography, page 3; Getty Images, pages 1 and 50; Image reproduced with the kind permission of J.C. Bamford Excavators Limited with whom copyright in the image vests, page 60 (bottom); Stefan Marjoram, page 54-55; Mark Read, page 56; Howard Statham, page 49; Chris Yates, page 58.

All other images (including the front and back cover pictures) courtesy National Motor Museum, Beaulieu, whose kind assistance is gratefully acknowledged.

CONTENTS

THE BEGINNING

FROM THE DAYS of horse-drawn transport to the steam era, and then to the motorcar and motorcycle, humans have strived to travel ever faster. Once motorised transport had become our preferred means of getting about independently, very soon the idea of travelling from one place to another turned to 'how fast can we get there?' Mankind's fascination with speed had found a new arena in which challenges could be set and records broken.

The race to be the fastest motorist was on, and the land speed record was born. Initially, the record was a timed event

'Jeantaud' was driven by Comte Gaston de Chasseloup-Laubat to the first official land speed record.

'La Jamais Contente' with Camille Jenatzy at the wheel. He was nicknamed the 'Red Devil' due to his wild red hair. He broke the record three times.

over a measured 1-kilometre straight flat road in whichever direction required, and the speed was calculated. This was changed to a two-way average in 1914, with a maximum of one hour allowed between the moment you entered the starting point and the moment you reached the same point on the return journey. Generally, for the outright world land speed record, the distance is either the mile or the kilometre.

In November 1898 the Automobile Club de France (ACF) sponsored a hill climb at Chanteloup near Paris. Fifty-four cars took part, mostly electrically driven. The race was won by a Belgian, Camille Jenatzy, at 18mph in his electric car.

He had beaten the local favourite, Comte Gaston de Chasseloup-Laubat, who was driving a locally built electric car from the Jeantaud Electric Motor Company. These early vehicles were known as CGA dogcarts and had heavy lead acid batteries.

Chasseloup-Laubat, being a founder member of the ACF, secretly requested a new event to be organised in Agricole Park, Achères, Saint Germain, north of Paris. A 1.2-mile course was prepared and on 18 December 1898 the first

Léon Serpollet at Bexhill in 1902 with his steam-powered 'Oeuf de Pâques' or 'Easter Egg'.

world land speed record was established by the Comte in his Jeantaud 36hp electric car with a speed of 39.24mph over the flying kilometre. He had beaten all his rivals (including the new petrol internal combustion engine cars) except Jenatzy, who was unable to attend. The Jeantaud was fitted with the world's first steering wheel, horizontally mounted, rather than a tiller, like all the other cars had.

Jenatzy immediately took up the challenge and on 17 January 1899 the two met at Achères in an electric car 'duel'. Jenatzy raised the record to 41.42mph. However, the Comte instantly replied with a speed of 43.69mph for his second record. The battle had worn out the batteries in each car, so both had to call it a day!

On 27 January 1899 Jenatzy returned to Achères on his own and increased the record to 49.92mph. The Comte's initial retort was beset by mechanical and weather issues, but he returned on 4 March with the addition of a pointed nose

and tail to 'Jeantaud'. The drivers still sat perched on top of their cars, adding hugely to the aerodynamic drag. This time he increased the record by just under 7mph to 57.60mph.

In the meantime Jenatzy was busy with building the world's first land speed 'Special', a car built for the single objective of breaking the record, christened 'La Jamais Contente' ('The Never Satisfied'). Looking a bit like a cigar on wheels, it represented a basic attempt at streamlining. On 29 April, he increased the record to 65.79mph and became the first person to exceed 100km/h at a speed of 105km/h.

A new competitor entered the fray in 1902: Frenchman Léon Serpollet and his egg-shaped steam-powered car, 'Oeuf de Pâques' ('Easter Egg'). During the speed week held on the Promenade des Anglais on 13 April he increased the record to 75.06mph. This record was exactly matched by Baron Pierre de Caters in July in his petrol-driven French-built Mors.

Baron de Caters went on to break the record in this Mercedes in 1904, having exactly equalled Serpollet's speed in 1902.

Henry Ford and Barney Oldfield with the Ford 'Arrow 999' in January 1904. Ford chose a frozen lake for his attempt but the speed of 91.37mph was not recognised by the French authorities. Hot cinders were spread along the course!

The first petrol engine able to claim the record was a Mors, driven by American millionaire William K. Vanderbilt on 5 August 1902 at a speed of 76.08mph on a road at Ablis in north-central France.

The rush was now on to be the fastest man on Earth: on 5 November Henri Fournier driving a Mors pushed the record up to 76.60mph, which was then beaten on 17 November by M. Augières at Dourdan, also driving a Mors, at a speed of 77.13mph.

In the early days of these records there were no rules on how much a previous record must be beaten by, so the record could be pushed up by the smallest of margins.

Also at Dourdan, in early 1903 Arthur Duray broke the record twice at speeds of 83.47mph and 84.73mph in his French-built Gobron-Brillié.

Henry Ford now took an interest, wanting to promote his latest model prior to the New York Motor Show.

The first car to break the 100mph barrier, a Gobron-Brillié driven by Louis Rigolly in Ostend on 21 July 1904.

On 12 January 1904, on the frozen Lake St Clair, Michigan, USA, he achieved 91.37mph driving the very basic Ford 'Arrow', which was more like an engine and seat attached to a chassis! However, this was not recognised by the French ACF because the timing equipment was not officially authorised.

William Vanderbilt also suffered at the hands of the French authorities: on Daytona Beach, Florida, he achieved 92.30mph, but his speed was also not recognised!

The next 'official' record-breaking run was on 31 March back on the Promenade des Anglais in Nice by Louis Rigolly driving a Gobron-Brillié at a speed of 94.78mph.

Having equalled the record in 1902, Baron Pierre de Caters broke the record at last with a speed of 97.25mph at Ostend in a Mercedes on 25 May 1904. He had set his heart on being the first to 100mph but was beaten to it by Rigolly taking his second record in his Gobron-Brillié on 21 July with a speed of 103.55mph, again at Ostend.

Rigolly held the record for only a few weeks before it was increased to 104.52mph by Paul Baras on 13 November in a Darracq, also at Ostend.

THE RACE TO 150MPH AND TO 3 MILES IN A MINUTE

ATTEMPTS ON DAYTONA Beach in 1905 by Arthur MacDonald and Herbert Bowden were still not officially recognised by the ACF. Back in Europe on 30 December 1905 Victor Hemery achieved 109.65mph in a V8 Darracq at Arles in France. Victor Hemery sold his 1909 Vanderbilt Cup-winning Darracq to Malcolm Campbell; this would become the first car named 'Blue Bird'.

Steam made a brief but spectacular appearance in 1906 with a Stanley Steamer driven by Fred Marriott. The Stanley Motor Company was producing hundreds of steam cars in America and they built the Stanley Steamer 'Rocket', shaped like an upturned canoe and painted red, with Fred Marriott seated in the middle. On Daytona Beach he increased the record by just over 12mph to 121.57mph over the measured kilometre and it became the first vehicle to achieve the milestone of travelling at over two miles in a minute! His mile speed was recorded as 127.60mph but for some reason was not ratified in Paris.

A return to Daytona in 1907 saw the car crash at over an estimated 140mph. Fred was thrown clear, but his eye became detached from its socket with the impact; luckily for him a passing doctor was able to pop the eye back with the aid of a teaspoon!

The internal combustion engine fraternity were taken by surprise with the performance of their steam-powered competitor and it was not until three years later that the record was broken again.

OPPOSITE: Malcolm Campbell sitting in the Sunbeam 350hp with mechanic Leo Villa in the background.

Arthur MacDonald with Napier L48 reached 104.65mph on Daytona Beach in 1905, but the speed was not recognised by the French authorities.

The attention was switching from Europe to Britain with the emergence of the Brooklands race track at Weybridge in Surrey, the first purpose-built circuit in the world. It was built in 1907 by Hugh Locke King in the grounds of his estate at huge expense, which nearly bankrupted him. The track, made of concrete, was 2¾ miles long and 100 feet wide, with two long straights joined by two sections of 30-foot-high banked curves. On 8 November 1909 Victor Hemery, driving a 220bhp Benz, pushed the record up to 125.95mph.

The Stanley Steamer 'Rocket' driven by Fred Marriot at 121.57mph in 1906 on Daytona Beach.

The Americans continued to claim new records but the ACF did not officially recognise them due to the timing equipment used. Barney Oldfield claimed 131.27mph in his 'Blitzen Benz' on Daytona Beach on 16 March 1910 and Bob Burman, also driving a Benz, claimed 141.37mph on 23 April 1911.

Until now the records had been timed in whichever direction best suited the conditions. However, a new rule was introduced by the ACF to negate any advantages of a

The wreck of the Stanley 'Rocket' on Ormand Beach, Daytona, in 1907. The driver, Fred Marriott, survived this crash at an estimated 140mph.

Aerial photograph of the Brooklands circuit in 1939, showing the Campbell road racing circuit cutting across the infield.

In 1914 the first two-way average record was set by L.G. Hornstead in the 'Blitzen Benz' on the Brooklands race track in Surrey, UK.

favourable wind or slope conditions. Competitors were now timed over a two-way run on the same course in opposite directions within one hour of each other and the average of the two runs gave the new speed. The first competitor to set a record with these new rules was L.G. Hornstead, driving a 250bhp Benz on 24 June 1914 at Brooklands with an average speed of 124.10mph. His two runs showed how much the gradient and wind affected the speeds: one run was 128.16mph; the other was 120.28mph.

After the First World War there was a surplus of big aero engines and the race was on to be the first to achieve 150mph. The Americans continued to claim records, but these were still not officially recognised by the ACF.

Kenelm Lee Guinness, the inventor of KLG spark plugs, increased the record to 133.75mph on 17 May 1922 back on the Brooklands circuit. His car, the 350hp V12 Sunbeam, attracted the attention of none other than fellow Brooklands competitor Captain Malcolm Campbell. This was also the last time that Brooklands was used as a venue for the outright land speed record.

The first record after the First World War was broken by Kenelm Lee Guinness, seen here at Brooklands race track driving the Sunbeam 350hp.

The battle temporarily returned to France, and for the last time on a public road in Arpajon. Frenchman René Thomas and Englishman Ernest Eldridge duelled for the record. On 6 July 1924 René was driving a twelve-cylinder racing Delage and set a speed of 143.31mph. Eldridge's car was also a track racing car but a Fiat named 'Mephistopheles II', with a massive Fiat aero engine. However, it lacked a reverse gear and was reported by Thomas to the authorities and Eldridge was not allowed to compete until six days later. On 12 July, with the addition of the reverse gear, he pushed the record up to 146.01mph.

It was during this time that Captain Malcolm Campbell had persuaded the Sunbeam Motor Company to allow him to drive, and eventually buy, the 350hp V12 Sunbeam. He was determined to get the record and be the first person to achieve 150mph. Attempts on the sand at Saltburn, and two visits to the speed trials on a beach at Fanoe, Denmark, yielded no success, however, and also claimed the life of a small boy when a detached tyre crashed into the watching crowd on the beach.

He then chose Pendine Sands in Carmarthenshire, Wales – a 7-mile compacted sand beach – and on 25 September

A determined Captain Malcolm Campbell broke his first records on Pendine Sands in the 350hp Sunbeam. His first record was 146.16mph and then 150.76mph.

1924 he managed to increase the record by one of the smallest increments in history to 146.16mph. He returned on 21 July 1925 with the addition of a longer streamlined tail and became the first person to drive at 150mph, establishing a new record of 150.76mph.

The Sunbeam had broken three records and was now at its limit; next, Malcolm set about building his first purpose-built

The Sunbeam 'Tiger', with Henry Segrave driving on Southport Beach in 1926.

'Blue Bird'. In the meantime there was a rush on for three miles a minute, or 180mph, as the next target. Sunbeam replied with a new car for their 'works' Grand Prix driver, Major Henry Segrave. Driving the Sunbeam 'Tiger' with a small chassis and a V12 4-litre engine on Southport beach on 16 March 1926, Segrave pushed the record up to 152.33mph.

The record now caught the attention of Welshman J.G. Parry-Thomas, a successful racing driver at Brooklands who also happened to be a very talented engineer. He bought the 'Higham Special' from Count Louis Zborowski. The power source was a massive American Liberty 400hp V12 engine. He re-christened the car 'Babs', after his mother, and on Pendine Sands on 27 April 1926 he achieved 169.30mph. The following day he went even faster, pushing the speed to 171.02mph.

Parry-Thomas's 'Babs' having a wheel changed on Pendine Sands, where he broke the record on 27 April 1926 and increased it the next day. He lost his life in 1927 attempting to get the record back.

Parry-Thomas's 'Babs' on Pendine Sands preparing for a run.

Parry-Thomas set about making modifications to improve his speed, while both Campbell and Segrave were preparing new vehicles to wrestle the record back. On 4 February 1927 Campbell was the first to appear, and back on Pendine Sands took the record back with a speed of 174.88mph. This was an eventful attempt: Malcolm had his goggles ripped from his face as he tried to see through a sand- and seawater-splashed windshield screen!

The new, mighty, twin aero engine 1,000hp 'Red Slug' was now on its way to Daytona Beach and expected to perform very well when Henry Segrave took the wheel. Parry-Thomas felt under pressure, and he knew that his car could only achieve 180–190mph. He arrived on Pendine Sands on 3 March with a heavy cold and was travelling at about 180mph when (as it was reported at the time) the drive chain snapped and because he was leaning out of the cockpit, Brooklands-style, he was decapitated. The car was buried under the sands until it was exhumed and restored by a Mr Wyn Owen, at which point

evidence came to light that the crash might have been caused by a broken wheel. 'Babs' can be seen today attending classic race meetings around the UK. Parry-Thomas's death shocked the racing world; this was the first driver fatality and it confirmed the dangers of the game to all who competed in it.

Parry-Thomas's company, Thomas Inventions Development Co. Ltd, had been based at Brooklands, in partnership with Major Ken Thomson. After his death, Thomson carried on, joined by Ken Taylor, under the new name of Thomson & Taylor. Reid Railton, who had previously worked for Parry-Thomas, joined as Technical Director and Designer, and the company went on to have an important influence on the land speed record in the 1930s, not only in terms of the design work of Reid Railton but also with the building of bodywork panels for Malcolm Campbell's 'Blue Birds' and John Cobb's 'Railton Special'.

Captain Malcolm Campbell on Pendine Sands at 170mph in February 1927 with the first purpose-built 'Blue Bird'. Unable to see, he is wiping the windshield with his hand.

BRITISH DOMINATION

WHILE EN ROUTE TO Daytona, Segrave heard the terrible news of Parry-Thomas's death and was concerned about the chains on his Sunbeam – he sat between the two Matabele aero-engines, one ahead and one behind, using chain drive!

On 29 March 1927 Segrave breezed past the record and became the first person to travel at over 200mph. His new record of 203.79mph had beaten the record by the biggest official increase in history. However, he did not have it all his own way: on one run he was blown off course and on another he had to drive into the sea to cool his brakes.

A year later, in March 1928, Campbell returned to Daytona with a new, remodelled 'Blue Bird', and found himself in the middle of an American–English sandwich! Two American contenders arrived on the scene, Frank Lockhart, with his Stutz 'Black Hawk', and Ray Keech driving the 'White Triplex'.

The 'Black Hawk' was a very low-to-the-ground, streamlined, bullet-shaped car with two Miller straight-eight racing engines linked to form a supercharged V16. Malcolm Campbell was very impressed with the simplicity and its beautiful shape; he also greatly admired Frank Lockhart as a racer, who had won the Indianapolis 500 in 1926 at his first attempt. However, the same could not be said of the 'White Triplex'! It had three Liberty aero V12 engines, one in front of Keech and the other two to the side and slightly behind him. All this was placed onto a truck chassis with limited bodywork

OPPOSITE: Malcolm Campbell sitting in the 1927 version of 'Blue Bird' with a young Donald Campbell by his side.

Major Henry Segrave on Daytona Beach with the mighty twin-engine Sunbeam 1,000hp 'Slug' (the name was of course due to its shape: for the first time the body shell, painted red, now surrounded all four wheels).

save for a chisel-shaped nose and basic bodywork to surround the driver and engines; pure grunt would make this car work! However, the official scrutineers failed it, as it did not have a reverse gear; initially an electric motor and roller drive were unsuccessfully fitted onto a tyre, but this was unable to rotate the wheel due to the compression of the three large engines. A very complicated separate rear axle was fitted with its own driveshaft and system to lower the whole device to show it could reverse – this was removed for the record attempts!

Lockhart was the first to run, but a sudden gust of wind pushed the 'Black Hawk' into the sea. He had to be rescued by a human chain, who waded out chest deep to retrieve him. Keech ended up with a bad burn when a water hose broke; he also suffered with the effects of exhaust flames on another run. Malcolm Campbell was successful and increased the record to 206.96mph, his first above 200mph and setting him on his way towards his goal of 300mph.

Frank Lockhart in his compact Stutz 'Black Hawk'. Lockhart was a successful racing driver and talented engineer, but was killed in April 1928 during his second attempt on the record.

In April a patched-up Ray Keech returned and increased the record to 207.55mph; Frank Lockhart's attempt to reach 200mph ended in disaster, however, as he was killed when a tyre burst, turning the Stutz over.

Concerned about conditions on Daytona after Lockhart's accident, Malcolm Campbell was looking for a new venue to break records on and took a modified 'Blue Bird' car to Verneuk Pan in South Africa in 1929. He also knew that

The 'White Triplex' driven by Ray Keech on Daytona Beach, showing the extra rear wheel axle added to enable the car to reverse and qualify as a contender. Lee Bible was later killed in the same car.

The 'Golden Arrow' on Daytona Beach in 1929, streamlined by Irving and powered by a Napier Lion. It was the least-used record breaker with less than 20 miles on the clock.

Sunbeam and Segrave had a new, beautifully sleek car called 'Golden Arrow' arriving in Daytona, which was capable of speeds beyond what 'Blue Bird' could achieve.

Malcolm's fears were confirmed when Segrave easily increased the record to 231.45mph on 11 March 1929. The 930bhp Napier Lion aero engine of 'Golden Arrow' only needed two runs and is credited with less than 20 miles on the clock for its record attempts! Henry Segrave was knighted for his fabulous achievement. Meanwhile, Malcolm Campbell focused his attention on long-distance records, knowing that the outright land speed record was beyond him and the current 'Blue Bird'.

One of the mechanics of the 'White Triplex', Lee Bible, was invited to drive the car, as Ray Keech had refused to drive it again on safety grounds. Lee Bible had no previous experience with the car and after reaching just over 200mph he lifted off the accelerator too suddenly. The car went into a slide and threw Bible out, killing him instantly. It ended up in the sand dunes, also killing a Pathé news photographer, Charles Traub.

In March 1930 a new car from Sunbeam, the 'Silver Bullet', appeared on the beach at Daytona, driven by Englishman Kaye Don. However, this was not as successful as its predecessors from Sunbeam: a problem with its supercharger resulted in no records.

Sunbeam 'land speed' car, with Brooklands regular Kaye Don at the wheel. The car never achieved its full potential.

On Friday 13 June 1930 Sir Henry Segrave was killed on Lake Windermere attempting to break his own water speed record of 98.76mph in *Miss England II*. The death of his friend and British adversary left the way open for Malcolm Campbell, especially as the Americans were still hurting from the recent tragedies.

In February 1931 Malcolm Campbell revisited Daytona Beach with a new, modified and sleeker 'Blue Bird'; with its 1,450bhp supercharged 12-cylinder Napier Lion engine, Campbell achieved a new record of 246.09mph. Conditions were far from ideal, but this attempt only took a total of five minutes, as he did not stop for fresh tyres to complete the return run. Upon his return to Britain he was knighted for his achievement.

Malcolm
Campbell's 1931
modified 'Blue
Bird', with a
Rolls-Royce V12
R-type installed.

A year later Sir Malcolm was back on Daytona. 'Blue Bird' had a new nose and some gearbox improvements and he was able to increase his record beyond 250mph to 253.97mph. He also increased the 5-mile, and 5- and 10-kilometre distance records.

During the summer of 1932 'Blue Bird' acquired a new engine (a supercharged Rolls-Royce R-type engine V12 36.5 litre giving 2,300bhp), a modified body and a new clutch. Returning to Daytona again on 22 February 1933, Sir Malcolm added 20mph to his record, reaching the average of 272.46mph. He also increased the 5-kilometre record to 257.295mph.

The ambition to break 300mph was getting closer. Reid Railton was tasked with remodelling 'Blue Bird' to have a chance of this, and the car was extensively rebuilt. The R-type engine was kept but was going to drive twin rear wheels. A new wheel-enveloping body was designed, and a broad, full-width nose with a slot for the radiator that could be closed for extra speed in the measured mile. 'Blue Bird' now weighed 5 tons, with extra lead to help reduce wheel spin on Daytona.

After eight weeks of waiting for the weather to give a suitable beach, on 7 March 1935 Sir Malcolm had a torrid attempt on a less-than-ideal beach. He increased his old record by only 4mph to 276.82mph. Bitterly disappointed, but still determined to realise 300mph, he sought a new venue to replace Daytona.

Sir Malcolm returned to America but this time to the Bonneville Salt Flats, a massive dried up salt lake in Utah. On 3 September 1935 Malcolm achieved his goal with an average of 301.129mph. It was not easy going: tyres burst and caught alight, when the radiator was closed off the screen was covered with oil, and choking fumes filled the cockpit. The timekeepers also made an initial error with their calculations but corrected them later to give him the record.

Sir Malcolm then retired from land speed to focus on water speed, and went on to break four world water speed records.

Further modifications to 'Blue Bird' in 1935 only added a slight increase to the old record on Daytona Beach.

To Leo Villa
A True Friend
From Malcolm Campbell

"Our Ambition at last achieved."

Speed 301·1 mph
3ᵈ September 1935
Salt

'Our Ambition at last' – Malcolm Campbell's finest achievement was 301mph on the Bonneville Salt Flats, Utah, USA, on 3 September 1935.

He used the same Rolls-Royce R-type engine (numbered R37) from the 'Blue Bird' car to power the *Blue Bird K3* boat, but R37 overheated during a high-speed run and the R39 was installed to achieve the water speed record. Unlike many other drivers, he passed away from natural causes in 1948 after a series of strokes.

It is worth mentioning here that the same British-made Rolls-Royce R-type is the only engine to hold all three records, on land, on water and in the air: the air speed record in 1929 with the Supermarine S6 flown by Squadron Leader Augustus Henry Orlebar CBE AFC & Bar (Air Force Cross); the water speed record with Sir Henry Segrave in *Miss England II* on Lake Windermere in 1930; and the land speed record with Sir Malcolm Campbell in 'Blue Bird' in 1933. In total, the engine won two Schneider Trophy air races, nine world water speed records and three world land speed records.

THE LAST WHEEL-DRIVEN RECORDS

THE BRITISH CONTINUED their domination of the land speed record, first with Captain George Eyston MC (Military Cross) and his new massive 7-ton monster car called 'Thunderbolt', which had two R-type engines driving twin rear wheels and four wheels at the front in pairs, all steering. On 19 November 1937 on Bonneville he increased the record to 312.00mph. The following year on 27 August he pushed the record up to 345.50mph.

Then another Brooklands racing driver, John Cobb, entered the arena with his futuristic teardrop-shaped 'Railton Special'. Designed by Reid Railton, it used two Napier Lion engines

Captain George Eyston in his 'Thunderbolt'. His first record was 312.00mph in November 1937. In this picture he is sitting in the 1938 modified version.

Captain George Eyston increased his record to 345.5mph again on Bonneville in 'Thunderbolt' in August 1938. John Cobb bettered that record and a day later Eyston pushed the record up to 357.50mph.

to drive the four wheels. An S-shaped chassis was utilised to accommodate the two engines, one driving the back wheels and the other driving the front. On 15 September 1938 Cobb achieved 350.20mph. A day later, George Eyston (with the addition of a big tailfin on 'Thunderbolt' for straight-line stability) was able to push the record up to 357.50mph.

George Eyston, awarded the OBE in 1948, was also a prolific endurance record breaker in various classes and over various distances ranging from 1 hour to 24 hours and 1 kilometre to 1,000 miles with his cars 'Speed of the Wind' and 'Flying Spray'. An endurance record that still stands was in a car built from an AEC (Associated Equipment Company) diesel engine from a Routemaster bus fitted into a car with a Chrysler chassis. On the race track at Linas-Montlhéry, France, Eyston broke the standing start distance records from 1 hour 105.60mph to 24hrs, 1 kilometre to 1,000 miles averaging 99.10mph in Category A Group 3 Class 13. George Eyston passed away on 11 June 1979 still holding many other class records.

On 23 August 1939, nine days before the outbreak of the Second World War, John Cobb went on to 369.70mph. Cobb returned to Bonneville on 16 September 1947 with a

rebuilt 'Railton Special'. His average speed over two runs was 394.20mph, and he had a best one-way average of 403.13mph, the first car to go past 400mph. John Cobb went on to attempt the water speed record, but on 29 September 1952 was killed on Loch Ness in his jet-powered boat *Crusader*.

John Cobb with his team and the very sleek teardrop-shaped 4-wheel-drive 'Railton Special'.

During the 1950s Malcolm's son Donald Campbell had been breaking the water speed record with his jet hydroplane boat *Bluebird K7*. He turned his attention to the land speed record towards the end of the 1950s, commissioning the

John Cobb's 'Railton Special' held the record from 1939 until 1964 after increasing it in 1948 to 394.20mph.

The 'Flying Caduceus', the world's first jet car, driven by Dr Nathan Ostich on Bonneville in 1960. While no record was broken, it did give a foretaste of what was to come.

Norris brothers, who had designed *Bluebird K7*, to design him a car that followed the rules as laid down by the FIA (Fédération Internationale de l'Automobile) – the car had to have four wheels and be driven by at least two wheels. The new 'Bluebird CN7' was powered by a Bristol Siddeley Proteus gas turbine, which drove all four wheels. It was designed to achieve 450mph (with secret hopes of 500mph) and had massive wheels to stop the centrifugal force taking the rubber off the tyres.

Donald Campbell arrived on Bonneville in August 1960 to find a competitive field of American challengers, namely Art Arfons in 'Green Monster', Athol Graham in 'City of Salt Lake', Mickey Thompson in 'Challenger 1' (with four Pontiac V8s driving all four wheels), and lastly Dr Nathan Ostich in the first jet car, the 'Flying Caduceus' with 7,000lb of thrust. First to run was Athol Graham, a Mormon preacher, in his V12 supercharged Allison aero engine car. He had already achieved 344mph in December 1959 and despite concerns about the construction of the car voiced by Mickey Thompson, and a high crosswind, Graham went ahead. He accelerated too hard on his first run, breaking the rear suspension from a Cadillac road car, which was too weak for the forces involved. The car

yawed off course and rolled, landing upside down and killing Graham, who had not worn seatbelts.

Art Arfons withdrew after a couple of runs and two mechanical failures (including one to his parachute!), and Ostich encountered a number of problems with his jet car, including a grabbing brake, steering and fuel pump. He withdrew for a rethink, but the die was cast for the future.

Mickey Thompson fared slightly better with a best one-way speed of 406.60mph; however, on his return run a driveshaft broke, ending that attempt. He tried again but experienced other mechanical failures before bad weather led to a deterioration of the salt conditions.

Donald Campbell felt the strain; he had turned up with a big team and the world's most expensive motorcar. He had seen the relatively easy speed of Mickey Thompson, Athol Graham's accident and the dawn of the jet car. After some low-speed test runs Donald was keen to impress and on his fifth run he accelerated much harder from the start; at about 350mph 'Bluebird' left the prepared course, leapt into the air and continued a series of rolls and bounces for over half a mile. Donald survived with a fractured skull and perforated eardrum, saved by his safety harness and the

Mickey Thompson would have broken the record in 'Challenger I' but was robbed by a broken wheel bearing on the return run. His outward run was 406.6mph.

Leo Villa played a vital part of the Campbell story, being the mechanic for both Malcolm and Donald Campbell, but also being a good friend to Donald. Leo, seen here with 'Bluebird CN7', passed away in 1979.

integral strength of the car designed by the Norris brothers. Donald immediately announced his intention to have another go from his hospital bed and set about a complete rebuild. In the meantime the Americans continued the race to 400mph. Nathan Ostich continued the chase but with little success. Another fatality on the salt in 1962 reminded everyone of the dangers: Glenn Leasher was killed driving 'Infinity'. Having achieved 330mph, he announced he was ready to have a crack at 400mph, despite advice from the officials to have some more slow speed runs. He, like others before, was impatient and accelerated away too quickly and at 250mph the car up-ended itself and crushed the unfortunate Leasher, who sat forward of the front wheels.

All three crashes had impatience and the lack of a tailfin in common. The rebuilt 'Bluebird' inherited a big tailfin to help with straight-line stability.

The year 1963 saw the introduction of Craig Breedlove to the world of record-breaking, a Californian hot-rodder. His 'Spirit of America' achieved 407.45mph, but this was not recognised by the FIA, as it had three wheels and was a thrust vehicle. Eventually the FIA agreed to set up a new category for thrust vehicles. Effectively this ended the wheel-driven car as a contender for the outright record.

Donald Campbell carried on with his attempts with the rebuilt 'Bluebird CN7'. He found a new dried salt lake in Australia called Lake Eyre. He continued against the odds

Donald Campbell and 'Bluebird CN7', seen here in 1963 on Lake Eyre as the flood levels rose and the team had to abandon the attempt for another year.

Donald Campbell standing in front of 'Bluebird CN7' with his pipe.

Donald Campbell increased the record to 403.10mph on 17 July 1964 and this was the last time that a wheel-driven car held the outright record.

to break the record in the knowledge that the American jet cars would soon easily overtake the maximum potential of 'Bluebird'. The first attempts in 1963 were washed away with the first rains in seven years.

The team returned in 1964 and just as trial runs began the rains returned. However, in an act of great bravery on 17 July, Donald managed to achieve a new record with an average of 403.10mph on a surface that was breaking up underneath him as the flood waters returned. At last he had broken the record – but not at the speed he hoped for, and not faster than Breedlove. He knew that with the right conditions he and 'Bluebird' could go a lot faster. However, he switched to the world water speed record and became the first person to break both world records in the same year by raising his record to 276.33mph on water on 31 December on Lake Dumbleyung.

Donald Campbell CBE was later killed attempting to raise his world water speed record beyond 300mph. On 4 January 1967, at an estimated 320mph, his *Bluebird K7* boat took off and somersaulted after hitting his own wash from the outward journey.

Donald with Mr Whoppit, his lucky mascot; he was a very superstitious man. Donald was killed on Coniston Water on 4 January 1967 attempting 300mph.

The name 'Bluebird' passed from one car to another, from track racing to world speed records, from land to water, from father to son. In the passage of time, as world record succeeded world record, each became one more milestone of human progress, a single word in a book of human endeavour, a book, perhaps without an end. A book in which every man has something to write of his struggles, successes and failures on his ascent of the mountain of progress. But each can only go so far since the mountain has no summit, for it leads to the stars. It has to be climbed, for mankind cannot regress; he may pause momentarily, but there is no going back on the path of life.

Donald Campbell

A one-off display at the National Motor Museum of a 'nest of Bluebirds'. The first to 150mph was the Sunbeam 350hp; the first to 300mph was 'Blue Bird' in 1935; the first to 400mph was 'Bluebird CN7'.

THE JET AGE

DONALD CAMPBELL'S RECORD-BREAKING run in July 1964 was the last time that a car driven by its wheels held the outright record. It was broken on 2 October 1964 by a jet car called 'Wingfoot Express', built by Walt Arfons and powered by a 6,200lb thrust Westinghouse J46 triple jet engine. Walt was unable to drive his car due to a heart attack, so the engineer Tom Green took over, achieving a speed of 413.20mph. The attempts were not without their own dramas and surprised the LSR world with the new record!

Three days later Walt's younger brother Art took his now jet-powered 'Green Monster', with a General Electric 15,000lb thrust J79 engine, to a new record of 434.02mph. His return run was timed at 479mph, showing the car's true potential. The 'Green Monster' was a crude-looking but highly effective machine, due to the engineering genius of Art.

The record did not stand for long; on 13 October 1964, just eight days later, Craig Breedlove returned with a modified 'Spirit of America' fitted with two front wheels and a newly rebuilt J47 engine giving 5,700lb thrust. He easily increased the record to 468.72mph in just two quick passes along the Bonneville course. Two days later he returned and averaged 526.28mph. On his return run after exiting the measured mile his parachutes failed and only left with disc brakes designed to stop the car from 150–200mph, he drove off course, the brakes burnt out and he ran out of room. The car went through a row of telegraph poles, snapping one, took off over a road, and

OPPOSITE: Gary Gabelich added nearly 20mph to the record, raising it to 622.41mph on 23 October 1970.

The 'Wingfoot Express' was designed by Walt Arfons and driven by Tom Green on Bonneville to a speed of 413.20mph.

landed in a brine lake nose first with the tail sticking out like a discarded toy! Breedlove climbed to safety.

Another twelve days later, on 27 October, Art Arfons reappeared with his 'Green Monster' and increased the record to 536.71mph. In the space of one month the record had been beaten five times and increased by over 142mph.

The following year, 1965, saw the return to the salt of the two Arfons brothers and Craig Breedlove. Walt Arfons

'Green Monster' and Art Arfons claimed the record from his half-brother Walt (ten years apart, they operated independently, hardly ever talking to each other) and driver Tom Green after just three days, with a speed of 434.02mph.

Craig Breedlove with his three-wheeled 'Spirit of America' in which he achieved 407.45mph; it was not officially recognised as a car record, however.

built a new rocket-powered 'Wingfoot Express', driven by Bob Tatroe, who managed to get the car up to 476mph before a fire destroyed it. On 2 November Craig Breedlove revealed a new car, 'Spirit of America – Sonic 1', using another General Electric J79 jet engine, with 15,000lb thrust and a projected potential of 800mph. He increased the record to 555.48mph

Craig Breedlove and team with 'Spirit of America' on Bonneville.

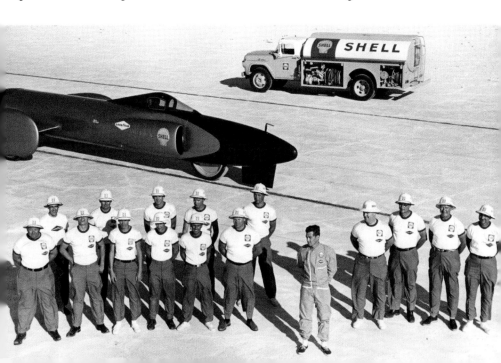

Art Arfons and 'Green Monster' on Bonneville. Art reclaimed the record from Craig Breedlove and managed to hold onto it this time for just over a year!

but again suffered a failed parachute and the tendency of the nose beginning to lift at high speed.

Five days later Art Arfons took 'Green Monster' back out and retorted with 576.55mph. However, on the return run after exiting the measured mile a rear tyre burst, ripping away one parachute and damaging the electrical firing mechanism for the second one. Arfons was unable to see, and with the cockpit now full of smoke, he veered off course and struck a

Craig Breedlove and 'Spirit of America – Sonic I' on Bonneville in 1964, in which he broke the record three times.

marker pole, ripping a front tyre and severely damaging the front bodywork. He smashed the cockpit glass and was able to steer back on course, pull the manual lever for the parachute and stop safely!

Craig Breedlove did not wait too long to give his reply. On 15 November he blasted down Bonneville in 'Spirit of America – Sonic 1' at an amazing 600.60mph. He still experienced the nose lifting, severe buffeting, and he could feel the frame flexing under him. This was the final act of 1965, as the weather changed and ended any further attempts.

During this great jet battle, two brothers – Bill and Bob Summers – appeared with their wheel-driven car 'Golden Rod'. They were after Donald Campbell's 403.1mph record. 'Golden Rod' was powered by four Chrysler V8 6.9-litre engines in a very low, sleek, narrow, pencil-shaped car. On 13 November 1965 Bob Summers achieved a new wheel-driven record of 409.27mph.

Art Arfons returned to Bonneville in 1966 with a modified 'Green Monster', a new rear suspension, and alterations to the nose and air intake, but still using the J79 jet engine. On 17 November, travelling at around 610mph, a wheel bearing seized, Arfons lost control, and the car cartwheeled and rolled several times, coming to rest some 4½ miles later. Amazingly,

'Golden Rod' and the Summers brothers at Bonneville, taking the wheel-driven record from Donald Campbell with a speed of 409.27mph on 13 November 1965.

'Wingfoot
Express', this
time powered by
solid-fuel rockets,
was once again
designed by
Walt Arfons and
driven by Bob
Tatroe. The car
was destroyed by
a fire.

Arfons survived with only cuts to his face, but 'Green Monster' was destroyed. Almost immediately he started planning for a new 'Green Monster' capable of breaking the next major target – the sound barrier.

Walt Arfons had been working on a new 'Wingfoot Express', this time powered by rockets – in fact fifteen jet-assisted take-off rockets, or 'JATO'. Initially Bob Tatroe achieved a standing mile record of 247.59mph with a top speed of 406.4mph. A redesign saw a total of twenty-five rockets installed, fifteen in the tail and five on each side. The attempt ended in failure when two rockets fell out and badly burnt the car. Three days later in a repaired car Bob Tatroe achieved an average 476.6mph with a one-way top speed of 580mph but the rockets were spent. Walt Arfons realised they were under-powered, but had shown that rocket power had great potential for the future.

In September 1970 another rocket car appeared at Bonneville. Reaction Dynamics Industries built 'The Blue Flame', a very long (38 foot), pencil-slim car, with two front wheels mounted very close to each other and the rear ones on outriggers 7 feet apart. The fuel was hydrogen peroxide giving 13,000lb of thrust or 35,000bhp! The original driver, Chuck Suba, was tragically killed in a dragster accident.

Gary Gabelich
and the
rocket-powered
'Blue Flame' on
Bonneville in
1970.

The replacement was Gary Gabelich, a NASA trainee and drag racer, and therefore an ideal pilot equipped to deal with the speeds and expected G forces.

After a series of tests and early problems, both with the car and internal team arguments, Gabelich and 'The Blue Flame' were ready on 23 October; he blasted down Bonneville at an average of 622.41mph. Unofficially, he had peaked at around 650mph, making him the fastest driver of any vehicle, beating the 632mph rocket-propelled sled of Lieutenant-Colonel J.P. Stapp.

Gabelich was subsequently badly hurt in his four-wheel-drive Funny Car at a drag meeting. His left hand was nearly torn off and left leg badly broken, but he made a steady recovery after many operations, and was due to drive another LSR rocket car designed by Bill Fredrick. Sadly, Gary Gabelich was killed in a motorcycle road accident on 26 January 1984 in San Pedro, California.

THE SOUND BARRIER

Bill Fredrick had been inspired by John Cobb's record of 394.20mph and was a consultant on the 'Blue Flame' attempt. His ambition was to break the speed of sound and had designed various cars in the past. Eventually he ended up with a similar looking vehicle to 'The Blue Flame' called 'SMI Motivator', powered by a hydrogen peroxide rocket giving 24,000lb of thrust with a top speed of 850mph. With this car, Hal Needham, a Hollywood stuntman and future movie writer and director, achieved a speed of 619.99mph on Bonneville on 14 October 1976. However, he overshot the prepared course, damaging the car and badly shaking himself!

On 6 December 1976 on the Alvord Desert in South Eastern Oregon, a new women's land speed record of 512.71mph was recorded by Kitty O'Neil, another stunt person. She beat the previous record set by Mrs Lee Breedlove, who had driven her husband's 'Sonic 1' to 308.56mph on 4 November 1965. O'Neil was a 3-metre and platform diving champion, and had been born deaf. She would have been at the Olympics but contracted spinal meningitis, and survived two treatments for cancer. She was only allowed to use 60 per cent of full power due to a contract that stipulated that only Hal Needham was entitled to challenge Gary Gabelich's record. On one run she had hit 618mph but had run out of fuel and was coasting the final part of the course. Hal Needham demanded his chance and during the ensuing legal dispute the weather closed in and they missed their opportunity to go for the record. It was very

likely that had she been allowed to continue, Kitty O'Neil would have broken the outright record, becoming the first female record-holder.

An interesting innovation to the SMI Motivator was the introduction of solid aluminium alloy wheels. Each was 32 inches in diameter and weighed 120lb, thereby removing the need for rubber and the risk of punctures.

After the legal squabbles and since 'SMI Motivator' had seemingly reached its peak, Bill Fredrick set about designing a new car. In 1979 the 'Budweiser Rocket' was born; it was another missile-shaped copy of 'The Blue Flame', with a very tight cockpit – hardly enough room for pilot Stan Barrett to breathe! The car featured two rear wheels on outriggers, with a 10-foot rear track and a single front wheel that was made from solid aluminium alloy. The power source was a Romatec V4 rocket.

The project was always going to cause controversy; it had three wheels and would qualify under FIM (Fédération International de Motocyclisme) rules for a motorcycle. It also could not achieve a return run due to insufficient fuel and it took longer to refuel than the one hour allowed. On 10 September 1979 Barrett reached a top speed on one run of

Stan Barrett and the 'Budweiser Rocket' claimed to have broken the sound barrier on Edwards Air Force Base in California on 17 December 1979. However, no sonic boom was recorded.

638.637mph on Bonneville and claimed it as a faster record than Gabelich's. As well as upsetting the purists, this run could not qualify for any official records.

Calculations showed that the car needed more thrust, so a sidewinder missile was added to the car, providing an extra 400–600lb of thrust. On 17 December 1979 on Rogers Dry Lake at Edwards Air Force Base in California, Stan Barrett and the 'Budweiser Rocket' were timed at 739.666mph over a distance of 52.8ft (1/100th of a mile) by the USAF with a radar system bounced off a satellite!

The team claimed it was the first car to break the sound barrier. However, nobody heard a sonic boom, the timing did not meet FIA regulations, the 'car' only had three wheels, it was not timed over a mile or a kilometre distance, and it did not make a return run. It was not recognised by the FIA and to most LSR purists it was little more than a publicity stunt. It was a very brave run by Stan Barrett and when asked about running again he replied, 'Heck, no, it means I still have another day to live!' The car did not run again.

'FOR BRITAIN AND FOR THE HELL OF IT' – RICHARD NOBLE

A young Richard Noble had seen John Cobb's jet hydroplane at Loch Ness in 1952 and was immediately hooked on record breaking. In 1974 he sold his Triumph TR6 to purchase an old Rolls-Royce Derwent Jet engine and set about designing and building his and Great Britain's first jet car – 'Thrust1', or as he described it, 'a cathedral on wheels'!

In March 1977, at RAF Fairford in Gloucester, travelling at approximately 200mph, a wheel bearing seized and pitched the car into a series of rolls. The car was destroyed, but Richard was unhurt. The remains of the car were sold for £175.

The new car 'Thrust2' was born, designed by John Ackroyd, resembling the 'Green Monster' with the cockpit placed alongside the engine and a passenger cockpit on the

other side! A Rolls-Royce Avon 302 turbojet, giving 17,000lb of thrust, was the power source and it ran on solid wheels. In September 1981, on Bonneville, Richard achieved 418.19mph before early rains flooded the course.

The team reassembled at Bonneville in 1982, but the rains returned. Richard was told of a possible surface at Black Rock Desert in Nevada and just six days later the team were repositioned! The new team manager was none other than Ken Norris, who had designed Donald Campbell's boat *Bluebird K7*, his car 'Bluebird CN7' and 'Bluebird CN8', a rocket car capable of 800mph but never built. Ken stated that the surface was the best he had seen for record attempts. After a series of runs and encountering a series of problems the fastest speed achieved was 590.55mph. The weather turned for the worse, but the team still needed to find more power. They returned in September 1983 for one final attempt. Rolls-Royce had re-tuned the engine, the underside of the bodywork was altered to reduce drag, and a new fuel system was fitted.

Richard Noble and 'Thrust2' brought the record back to Britain on 4 October 1983 with a speed of 633.47mph on the Black Rock Desert in Nevada. It is seen here on the RAF base at Thorney Island in 1983.

With 'Spirit of America – Sonic Arrow' Craig Breedlove hoped to break the sound barrier, but was fortunate to walk away from a 675mph crash on Black Rock Desert in 1996.

After a series of test runs, on 4 October, Richard Noble finally broke the record with a speed of 633.47mph. The record was back in British hands at last, after a nineteen-year break!

Back in America Art Arfons was still looking at breaking records. In 1989 he was on Bonneville but this time for an attempt to break the world motorcycle record with his 'Green Monster' number 27. However, all did not go to plan and this ended in failure after a high-speed roll.

He was back at Bonneville in October 1990; the motorcycle now had four wheels, two rear wheels fitted on outriggers. Again the attempt ended in failure after problems with the afterburner and severe vibrations from the wheels. Art finally retired from record breaking at this point, aged sixty-four years and a grandfather. He passed away on 3 December 2007 at the age of 81.

Craig Breedlove reappeared on Bonneville with a new contender, 'Spirit of America – Sonic Arrow', in August 1996. It was powered by a General Electric J79 jet engine from a US Navy F-4 Phantom jet plane, giving 22,650lb of thrust with an after burner thrust of 24,000lb.

The Bonneville surface was not in good condition and Craig could only manage speeds of around 360mph.

He reappeared on the Black Rock Desert and on 23 October he averaged 448mph, but storms cut short running that day. He increased his speed to 563mph on 27 October but again a storm curtailed further runs.

The next day Craig was timed at 470mph on his outward run. However, on the return at an estimated 675mph the left rear wheel suddenly lifted, turning the car on its left-hand side. 'Sonic Arrow' now did a wide left-hand 180-degree arc across the desert. Amazingly, Craig was unhurt and immediately planned to return in 1997.

In the meantime, in October 1996, Richard Noble and Andy Green had arrived on the Al-Jafr Desert in Jordan also with a new jet car called 'Thrust Super Sonic Car' or 'ThrustSSC'. It ran on four solid forged aluminium wheels, and was powered by two Rolls-Royce Spey jet engines, giving 110,000hp either side of the driver – Wing Commander Andy Green, an RAF fighter pilot.

The desert surface was rutted and harder than expected, causing problems, but speeds were increased slowly as part of a test program. However, bad weather forced the team home early having only achieved 325mph.

They returned in May 1997, but again there were problems with the course. After reaching 540mph the car suffered a major suspension failure. The team returned home due to the rising summer temperatures and the need for repairs.

Craig Breedlove returned to the Black Rock Desert and had started test runs on 4 September. Just two days later the 'ThrustSSC' team arrived on the desert, making their first test run on 8 September.

On 25 September 1997 Andy Green increased the record to 714.144mph, breaking Richard Noble's thirteen-year-old record by over 80mph – an amazing leap! He also managed to break the kilometre record still held by Gary Gabelich at 630.388mph, which Richard had just missed out on when he broke the mile record in 'Thrust2' back in 1983. On 6 October

it was Craig Breedlove's turn and he posted a run of 531mph; straight away Andy Green returned with two runs averaging 714mph and 727mph. The first unofficial supersonic run was on 7 October but it was not timed!

In a very generous gesture, Craig Breedlove had given the 'ThrustSSC' team his allotted time on the desert and allowed them to continue unhindered. On 13 October Andy Green drove at 749.876mph and returned at 764.168mph. However, it was outside the permitted time of one hour, by less than one minute!

Two days later, a double 'Boom' was heard across the desert as 'ThrustSSC' blasted through the outward mile at 759.333mph. The return run, this time within the permitted one hour, was timed at 771mph giving an average for both runs at 763.035mph. At last, the sound barrier had been officially beaten, a fantastic achievement by a small British Team with a big heart led by Richard Noble and driven by Andy Green. This was the biggest jump in the history of the Land Speed Record. Both Andy Green and Richard Noble were awarded the OBE (Order of the British Empire) in the 1997 honours list.

At the time of writing this is still the outright world land speed record. So, what does the future hold?

NEXT STOP: 1,000 MILES PER HOUR

CURRENTLY THERE ARE three main known challengers for the record: 'Aussie Invader', 'North American Eagle' and 'Bloodhound SSC'. A fourth contender would have been adventurer Steve Fossett, who purchased 'Spirit of America – Sonic Arrow' from Craig Breedlove. Unfortunately, Steve was killed on 3 September 2007 while flying his aircraft in Nevada. His remains were found in the mountains of Eastern Sierra Nevada a year after he went missing. Steve Fossett was the first person to fly solo non-stop around the world in a balloon.

'Aussie Invader 5R' is based in Perth, Australia, and will be driven by Rosco McGlashan, who was inspired by Donald Campbell's land speed attempts in 1964 on Lake Eyre.

In 1994, in 'Aussie Invader II', Rosco broke the Australian Land Speed Record at 500mph. This was Donald Campbell's 1964 wheel-driven record. 'Aussie Invader II' was powered by a 36,000hp Mirage jet fighter engine. Determined to go faster, and despite poor conditions and a concerned team Rosco set off on another attempt but at around 580mph the salt surface broke up and the resulting crash ended the attempt and the car was a write-off.

In 1996, with a new car, 'Aussie Invader III', powered by a SNECMA 9K-50 engine giving 19,000lb of thrust and 36,000hp, Roscoe reached 638mph one way, but could not make a return run due to bad weather. But for the changeable conditions, he might have been able to break

Bloodhound SSC with Andy Green during a test session on the runway at Newquay Airport achieving 200mph in under eight seconds, 26 October 2017.

Richard Noble's record! But once 'ThrustSSC' had raised the record, it was beyond the capabilities of 'Aussie Invader III'. In 1998 Rosco was awarded the Order of Australia Medal by Queen Elizabeth II for his services to motorsport and for his Australian Land Speed Record.

'Aussie Invader 5R', aiming for 1000mph, will be a rocket car with 62,000lb of thrust, a bi-propellant HTP (H2O2/hydogen peroxide) rocket motor giving an estimated 200,000hp! The car will run on four solid aluminium wheels. The car weighs 9.2 tonnes fully fuelled and is capable of accclerating from 0–1,000mph in just over 20 seconds, burning 2.8 tonnes of propellant! The team plan to run on Lake Gairdner, a dried lakebed in the state of South Australia.

The 'North American Eagle' project was started in 1998 by Ed Shadle and Keith Zanghi when they acquired an old

F-104 Star-fighter jet, stationed at Edwards Air Force Base in California. The aircraft was in a very bad state, fit for the scrap yard, and so started a long process of converting the aircraft into a contender for the land speed record. The J-79 engine generates over 42,500hp in full after burner, burning 90 gallons of aviation fuel per minute. The car weighs 7 tons, is 56 feet long and will run on solid aluminium wheels, two attached to the back of the old plane fuselage by outriggers and two close together just under the cockpit.

The team has two drivers, joint team owner Ed Shadle and Jessi Combs. Ed, now retired from working at IBM, owns his company E&D Services providing services to large data centres. A regular competitor on Bonneville, he is a member of the 200mph club with a record of 276.79mph in a lakester class car. Jessi, a TV personality and car racer, is aiming to

'Aussie Invader 5', the fifth version of Rosco McGlashan's, who holds the Australian land speed record, is aiming for 1,000mph.

break the women's land speed record of 512mph, currently held by Kitty O'Neil.

'Bloodhound SSC' follows in the wheel tracks of 'ThrustSSC' and is again led by the indomitable Richard Noble OBE and driven by Andy Green OBE, based in Bristol, UK. The design team is led by Chief Aerodynamicist Ron Ayers MBE (2014 New Year Honours for services to engineering), who was also involved with 'ThrustSSC' and the JCB 'Dieselmax'.

'Bloodhound SSC' will be powered by three very different engines. First, an EJ200 jet engine from a Eurofighter jet to get the car up to around 400mph and then a bespoke Nammo rocket. The third engine is a Jaguar Supercharged V8 and is used to drive the rocket oxidiser pump, in other words a V8 fuel pump!

The team will be making the attempts on Hakskeen Pan in the Northern Cape region of South Africa, which is a very hard and flat course, 19 kilometres long and 5 kilometres wide. The local Provincial Government is helping to prepare the new course by clearing tons of stones from the surface.

OTHER INTERNATIONAL CLASS RECORDS

'INSPIRATION' – STEAM CAR FIA CATEGORY A GROUP X CLASS 3

The British Steam Car took ten years from conception at Southampton University through to the international record on Edwards Air Force Base in August 2009. The project outgrew the University.

New team owner Charles Burnett III assembled a team based on his Hampshire estate to design and build the car. The official record to beat was still the Fred Marriott record set in 1906 of 121.57mph in the Stanley 'Rocket'. However, in 1985 on Bonneville an American team, with 'Steaming Demon' driven by Bob Barber, claimed the record at 145.607mph but they only achieved a one-way average.

The car weighed in at 3 tonnes and was 27 feet long (7.663m) with twelve boilers generating 3 megawatts of heat burning liquid petroleum gas. The resultant steam was squeezed along over 3km of tubing ending up spinning a two stage Curtis wheel turbine giving 360hp.

British steam car – 'Inspiration'. The fastest steam-powered car; a ten-year project, which saw Charles Burnett III achieve the record for the mile at 139.84mph and the author the kilometre with a speed of 148.30mph.

'Break my car or break my record'. The author is eternally grateful to Charles Burnett III for the opportunity to break the record for a car powered by steam.

The author was invited to be the test driver in 2007, and in 2009 went out with the team to Edwards Air Force Base in the Mojave Desert, California. After ten weeks of frustrating breakdowns and intense heat, on 23 August Charles Burnett III broke the record with an average of 139.843mph over the measured mile. In an amazing act of supreme generosity Charles said to the author, 'Don, to say "thank you" for all your efforts I want you to either break my car or break my record and go faster than the American speed of 145mph!' Luckily, on 25 August the car did not break and I broke the record with a speed of 148.308mph over the measured kilometre. I cannot thank Charles enough for his kindness!

WHEEL-DRIVEN RECORD CATEGORY A GROUP IX TURBINE ENGINE

Don Vesco, driving 'Turbinator' on 18 October 2001 on Bonneville, broke the record for a wheel-driven car with a speed of 458.44mph and the record still stands. Power is delivered to all four wheels by a 3,750hp engine tuned to give 4,400hp. On the return run a tyre burst at over 460mph, just as Vesco was exiting the measured mile, but he managed to control the car and bring it to a stop safely. His best one-way average was 470mph. Vesco started breaking records with his father's 1957 Model B Ford streamliner 'Little Giant', entering the prestigious 200mph club in 1963. He broke the motorcycle land speed record in 1978 in 'Lightning Bolt', powered by Kawasaki twin KZ1000 engines with a speed of 318.330mph. The record stood for over ten years and today stands at 376.36mph with the 'Ack Attack' streamliner driven/ridden by Rocky Robinson on Bonneville on 25 September 2010.

Don passed away in 2002 from cancer a year after setting his wheel-driven record and looking to achieve 500mph. His brother Rick, also a member of the Bonneville 200mph and 300mph club, has carried on with the project: a new car, 'Turbinator II', has been built with a more aerodynamic windscreen and smaller, more efficient air intakes. In 2016, with new driver Dave Spangler, a driveshaft broke at around 400mph causing another tyre blowout and body panels to fly off. Despite this, Dave brought the car to a safe stop. The car will be repaired and the project aim is still to break 500mph for a wheel-driven car.

'BUCKEYE BULLET' – ELECTRIC CAR FIA CATEGORY A GROUP VIII

'Venturi Buckeye Bullet 3' (VBB3) started life at the Ohio State University Centre for Automotive Research. It is a project run by the students, currently under the direction of faculty advisor Giorgio Rizzoni in partnership with the Monaco-based electric vehicle constructor, Venturi Automobile. The University has built a number of Buckeye Bullets with different power sources. They spent six years designing and building 'VBB3'. The car has two custom electric motors developed by Venturi, producing over two megawatts from lithium ion batteries. On 19 September 2016 driver Roger Schroer increased the record to 341.264mph on Bonneville. The aim of the programme is to see an electric car break 400mph.

The 'Venturi Buckeye Bullet 3' is the latest iteration in a series of electric racing vehicles built at Ohio State's Centre for Automotive Research, which has a 22-year history of

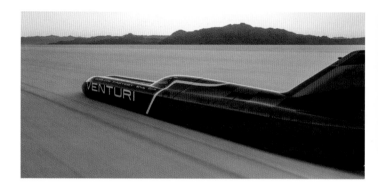

'Venturi Buckeye Bullet 3', currently the fastest electric car, driven by Roger Schroer at a speed of 341.264mph. The car is based at the Ohio State University and worked on by the students.

electric racing. In 2004, 'Buckeye Bullet 1', which ran on nickel metal hydride batteries, set a national land speed record with an average time of 315mph. 'Venturi Buckeye Bullet 2', the world's first hydrogen fuel cell-powered land speed electric vehicle, set the international record of 303mph in 2009.

'DIESELMAX' – DIESEL CAR FIA CATEGORY A

JCB 'Dieselmax Streamliner', the fastest diesel car, driven by Andy Green on Bonneville in 2006 to a speed of 350.092mph. Powered by two commercial JCB 140hp diesel engines tuned to produce 750hp.

The JCB 'Dieselmax Streamliner' was powered by two turbo-charged 750hp 'LSR' versions of the JCB444 140hp diesel engine, which is a standard engine used in JCB machines, driving four 23-inch Goodyear shod wheels. One engine drove the rear wheels and the other drove the front wheels. The 'Railton Special' of John Cobb used a similar set-up and was the inspiration for the design of the car. The team set their sights

on a target of 350mph; the driver was none other than Wing Commander Andy Green OBE with Richard Noble OBE as consultant and Ron Ayres MBE as the project aerodynamicist.

Andy eased the car to its first record on 18 August 2006 to 317mph and then increased it on 22 August 2006 to 328.767mph. The team were secretly hoping for 350mph, and this was achieved on 23 August with an outward run of 365mph and a return run of 335mph, giving the average 350.092mph for the mile and 350.452mph for the kilometre.

OTHER NOTABLE RECORDS
'MORMON METEOR'
Ab Jenkins still holds thirteen distance records ranging from 100km to 10,000km and 1 hour to 24 hours, set either in 1936 or 1940 on Bonneville. His 100-mile standing start record average is 190.670mph. The 10,000-kilometre record is 148.970mph.

'SPEED OF THE WIND/FLYING SPRAY'
Driven by Captain George Eyston, this car held two names and was powered by an un-supercharged version of the Rolls-Royce V12 Kestrel designed purely for endurance records. The car broke records in 1935 at 140.52mph and in 1936 at 149.096mph, but was destroyed during a bombing raid in the Second World War.

George Eyston OBE was a prolific record breaker in various classes and still holds fourteen official FIA records. Diesel car 'Flying Spray', 29 April 1936 on Bonneville.

FURTHER READING

Ackroyd, John. *Jet Blast and the Hand of Fate*. Red Line Books, 2007.

Bern-Campbell, Tonia. *My Speed King: Life with Donald Campbell*. Sutton Publishing, 2002.

Campbell, Gina. *Daughter of Bluebird*. Great Northern, 2012.

Campbell, Sir Malcolm. *My Thirty Years of Speed*. Hutchison & Co., c.1935.

Campbell, Sir Malcolm. *Speed on Wheels*. Sampson Low, Marston & Co Ltd, 1949.

Clarke, R.M. *The Land Speed Record 1898–1999*. Brooklands Books Ltd, 1999.

De Lara, David. *Leo Villa's Bluebird Album*. Transport Bookman Publications, 2007.

De Lara, David. *The Unobtainable: A Story of Blue*. David de Lara, 2014.

De Lara, David. *Donald Campbell: 300+ A Speed Odyssey*. History Press, 2016.

Holter, Steve. *Leap into Legend: Donald Campbell and the Complete Story of the World Speed Records*. Cambrian Printers, 2002.

Holthusen, Peter. *The Fastest Men on Earth: 100 Years of the Land Speed Record*. Sutton Publishing, 1999)

Jennings, Charles. *The Fast Set*. Little, Brown, 2004.

Posthumus, Cyril and Tremayne, David. *Land Speed Record: From 39.24 to 600+ mph*. Osprey Publishing, 1985.

Sheppard, Neil. *Donald Campbell: Bluebird and the Final Record Attempt*. The History Press, 2011.

Stevens, Donald. *Bluebird CN7*. Veloce Publishing Ltd, 2010.

Tremayne, David. *Donald Campbell: The Man Behind the Mask*. Transworld Publishers, 2004.

Varndell, Mike. *The British are Coming*. Transport Bookman Publications, 2011.

PLACES TO VISIT

Brooklands Museum, Brooklands Road, Weybridge, Surrey
KT13 0QN. Telephone: 01932 857381.
Website: www.brooklandsmuseum.com
Thinktank, Birmingham Science Museum, Millennium
Point, Curzon Street, Birmingham B4 7XG.
Telephone: 0121 348 8000.
Website: www.birminghammuseums.org.uk/thinktank
John Cobb's Railton Mobil Special.
Coventry Transport Museum, Millennium Place, Hales St,
Coventry CV1 1JD. Telephone: 024 7623 4270.
Website: www.transport-museum.com
National Motor Museum, John Montagu Building, Beaulieu,
Brockenhurst SO42 7ZN. Telephone: 01590 612345.
Website: www.beaulieu.co.uk *Bluebird CN7, Sunbeam
Golden Arrow, Sunbeam Red Slug and Sunbeam 350hp.*
Pendine Museum of Speed, Pendine, Carmarthen SA33 4NY.
Telephone: 01994 453488.
Website: www.carmarthenshire.gov.wales
Parry-Thomas's 'Babs' is an occasional visitor.
Lakeland Motor Museum, Old Blue Mill, Backbarrow,
Ulverston LA12 8TA. Telephone: 015395 30400.
Website: www.lakelandmotormuseum.co.uk
Campbell Bluebird display.
The Ruskin Museum, Coniston, Cumbria LA21 8DU.
Telephone: 01539 441164.
Website: www.ruskinmuseum.com
*The Bluebird wing with a Campbell display and the restored
Bluebird K7 when completed.*

INDEX